# SPEECH

OF

# HON. C. L. VALLANDIGHAM,

OF OHIO,

*Delivered in the House of Representatives, February* 20, 1861

WASHINGTON:
PRINTED BY HENRY POLKINHORN,
1861.

# The Great American Revolution of 1861.

---

The special order—namely, the report of the committee of thirty-three—being under consideration—

Mr. VALLANDIGHAM addressed the House as follows:

Mr. SPEAKER: It was my purpose, some three months ago, to speak solely upon he question of peace and war between the two great sections of the Union, and to efend at length the position which, in the very beginning of this crisis, and almost lone, I assumed against the employment of military force by the Federal Govern-nent to execute its laws and restore its authority within the States which might se-ede. Subsequent events have rendered this unnecessary. Within the three months r more, since the presidential election, so rapid has been the progress of events, and uch the magnitude which the movement in the South has attained, that the country as been forced—as this House and the incoming Administration will at last be forced, n spite of their warlike purposes now—to regard it as no longer a mere casual and emporary rebellion of discontented individuals, but a great and terrible REVOLUTION, which threatens now to result in permanent dissolution of the Union, and division nto two or more rival, if not hostile, confederacies. Before this dread reality, the trocious and fruitless policy of a war of coercion to preserve or to restore the Union as, outside, at least, of these walls and of this capital, rapidly dissolved. The peo-le have taken the subject up, and have reflected upon it, till to-day, in the South, lmost as one man, and by a very large majority, as I believe, in the North, and es-ecially in the West, they are resolved that, whatever else of calamity may befall us, hat horrible scourge of CIVIL WAR shall be averted. Sir, I rejoice that the hard Anglo-Saxon sense and pious and humane impulses of the American people have ejected the specious disguise of words without wisdom which appealed to them to nforce the laws, collect the revenue, maintain the Union, and restore the Federal uthority by the perilous edge of battle, and that thus early in the revolution they re resolved to compel us, their Representatives, belligerent as you of the Republican arty here may now be, to the choice of peaceable disunion upon the one hand, or Jnion through adjustment and conciliation upon the other. Born, sir, upon the soil f the United States; attached to my country from earliest boyhood; loving and evering her, with some part, at least, of the spirit of Greek and Roman patriotism; etween these two alternatives, with all my mind, with all my heart, with all my trength of body and of soul, living or dying, at home or in exile, I am for the Union which made it what it is; and therefore I am also for such terms of peace and ad-ustment as will maintain that Union now and forever. This, then, is the question which to-day I propose to discuss:—

HOW SHALL THE UNION OF THESE STATES BE RESTORED AND PRESERVED?

Sir, it is with becoming modesty and with something of awe, that I approach the liscussion of a question which the ablest statesmen of the country have failed to solve. But the country expects even the humblest of her children to serve her in this, the hour of her sore trial. This is my apology.

Devoted as I am to the Union, I have yet no eulogies to pronounce upon it to-day. It needs none. Its highest eulogy is the history of this country for the last seventy years. The triumphs of war and the arts of peace,—science; civilization; wealth; population; commerce; trade; manufactures; literature; education; justice; tran-quility; security to life, to person, to property; material happiness; common defense; national renown; all that is implied in the "blessings of liberty;" these, and more, have been its fruits from the beginning to this hour. These have enshrined it in the hearts of the people; and, before God, I believe they will restore and preserve it. And to-day they demand of us, their embassadors and representatives, to tell them how this great work is to be accomplished.

Sir, it has well been said that it is not to be done by eulogies. Eulogy is for times of peace. Neither is it to be done by lamentations over its decline and fall. These are for the poet and the historian, or for the exiled statesman who may chance to sit amid the ruins of desolated cities. Ours is a practical work; and it is the business of the wise and practical statesman to inquire first what the causes are of the evils for which he is required to devise a remedy.

Sir, the subjects of mere partisan controversy which have been chiefly discussed here and in the country, so far, are not the causes, but only the symptoms or developments of the malady which is to be healed. These causes are to be found in the nature of man and in the peculiar nature of our system of governments. Thirst for power and place, or preëminence—in a word, ambition—is one of the strongest and earliest developed passions of man. It is as discernible in the school-boy as in the statesman. It belongs alike to the individual and to masses of men, and is exhibited in every gradation of society, from the family up to the highest development of the State. In all voluntary associations of any kind and in every ecclesiastical organization, also, it is equally manifested. It is the sin by which the angels fell. No form of government is exempt from it; for even the absolute monarch is obliged to execute his power through the instrumentality of agents and ambition here courts one master instead of many masters. As between foreign States, it manifests itself in schemes of conquest and territorial aggrandizement. In despotisms, it is shown in intrigues, assassinations, and revolts. In constitutional monarchies and in aristocracies, it exhibits itself in contests among the different orders of society and the several interests of agriculture, trade, commerce, and the professions. In democracies, it is seen everywhere, and in its highest development for here all the avenues to political place and preferment, and emolument, too, are open to every citizen; and all movements and all interests of society, and every great question—moral, social, religious, scientific—no matter what, assumes, at some time or other, a political complexion, and forms a part of the election issues and legislation of the day. Here, when combined with interest, and where the action of the Government may be made a source of wealth, then honor, virtue, patriotism, religion, all perish before it. No restraints and no compacts can bind it.

In a Federal Republic all these evils are found in their amplest proportions, and take the form also of rivalries between the States; or more commonly or finally at least, especially where geographical and climatic divisions exist, or where several contiguous States are in the same interest, and sometimes where they are similar in institutions or modes of thought, or in habits and customs, of sectional jealousies and controversies which end always, sooner or later, in either a dissolution of the union between them, or the destruction of the federal character of the government. But however exhibited, whether in federative or in consolidated governments, or whatever the development may be, the great primary cause is always the same—the feeling that might makes right; that the strong ought to govern the weak; that the will of the mere and absolute majority of numbers ought always to control; that fifty men may do what they please with forty-nine; and that minorities have no rights, or at least that they shall have no means of enforcing their rights, and no remedy for the violation of them. And thus it is that the strong man oppresses the weak, and strong communities, states and sections, aggress upon the rights of weaker states, communities and sections. This is the principle; but I propose to speak of it to-day only in its development in the political, and not the personal or domestic relations.

Sir, it is to repress this principle that Governments, with their complex machinery, are instituted among men; though in their abuse, indeed, Governments may themselves become the worst engines of oppression. For this purpose treaties are entered into, and the law of nations acknowledged between foreign States. Constitutions and municipal laws and compacts are ordained, or enacted, or concluded to secure the same great end. No men understood this, the philosophy and aim of all just government, better than the framers of our Federal Constitution. No men tried more faithfully to secure the Government which they were instituting, from this mischief; and had the country over which it was established been circumscribed by nature to the limits which it then had, their work would have, perhaps been perfect, enduring for ages. But the wisest among them did not foresee—who indeed, that was less than omniscient could have foreseen?—the amazing rapidity with which new settlements and new States have sprung up, as if by enchantment, n the wilderness; or that political necessity or lust for territorial aggrandizement would, in sixty years, have given us new territories and States equal in extent to the entire area of the country for which they were then framing a Government? They were not priests or prophets to that God of MANIFEST DESTINY whom we now worship, and will continue to worship, whether united into one Confederacy still, or livided into many. And yet it is this very acquisition of territory which has given strength, though not birth, to that sectionalism which already has broken in pieces his, the noblest Government ever devised by the wit of man. Not foreseeing the evil or the necessity, they did not guard against its results. Believing that the great danger to the system which they were about to inaugurate lay rather in the ealousy of the State governments towards the power and authority delegated to the Federal Government, they defended diligently against that danger. Apprehending hat the larger States might aggress upon the rights of the smaller States, they provided that no State should, without its consent, be deprived of its equal suffrage in he Senate. Lest the legislative department might encroach upon the executive, hey gave to the President the self-protecting power of a qualified veto, and in turn nade the President impeachable by the two Houses of Congress. Satisfied that the everal State governments were strong enough to protect themselves from Federal ggressions, if, indeed, not too strong for the efficiency of the General Government, hey thus devised a system of internal checks and balances looking chiefly to the ecurity of the several departments from aggression upon each other, and to prevent he system from being used to the oppression of individuals. I think, sir, that the lebates in the Federal convention and in the conventions of the several States alled to ratify the Constitution, as well as the coteroporaneous letters and publications of the time, will support me in the statement that the friends of the Constiution wholly under-estimated the power and influence of the Government which hey were establishing. Certainly, sir, many of the ablest statesmen of that day arnestly desired a stronger Government; and it was the policy of Mr. Hamilton, nd of the Federal party which he created, to strengthen the General Government; nd hence the funding and protective systems—the national bank, and other similar chemes of finance, along with the "general-welfare doctrine," and a liberal contruction of the Constitution.

Sir, the framers of the Constitution—and I speak it reverently, but with the freeom of history—failed to foresee the strength and centralizing tendencies of the Federal Government. They mistook wholly the real danger to the system. They ooked for it in the aggressions of the large States upon the small States without egard to geographical position, and accordingly guarded jealously in that direction, iving for this purpose, as I have said, the power of a self-protecting veto in the enate to the small States, by means of their equal suffrage in that Chamber, and orbidding even amendment of the Constitution in this particular, without the conent of every State. But they seem wholly to have overlooked the danger of SECIONAL COMBINATIONS as against other sections, and to the injury and oppression f other sections, to secure possession of the several departments of the Federal Government, and of the vast powers and influence which belong to them. In ke manner, too, they seem to have utterly under-estimated SLAVERY as a disurbing element in the system, possibly because it existed still in almost every State; but chiefly because the growth and manufacture of cotton had scarce yet een commenced in the United States: because Cotton was not yet crowned ing. The vast extent of the patronage of the Executive, and the immense power nd influence which it exerts, seem also to have been altogether under-estimated. And independent of all these, or rather perhaps in connection with them, there were nherent defects incident to the nature of all governments; some of them peculiar o our system, and to the circumstances of the country, and the character of the eople over which it was instituted, which no human sagacity could have foreseen, ut which have led to evils, mischiefs, and abuses, which time and experience lone have disclosed. The men who made our Government were human; they *were* nen, and they made it for men of like passions and infirmities with themselves.

I propose now, sir, to inquire into the practical workings of the system; the expement—as the fathers themselves called it—after seventy years of trial.

No man will deny—no American at least; and I speak to-day to and for Americans—that in its results it has been the most successful of any similar Government ver established; and yet, in the very midst of its highest development and its perfect uccess, in the very hour of its might, while "towering in its pride of place," it has suddenly been stricken down by a revolution which it is powerless to control. S if I could believe, as the gentleman from Tennessee [Mr. ETHERIDGE] would see to have me believe, that for more than half a century the South has had all that s ever asked, and more than she ever deserved; and that now, at last, a few disco tented spirits have been able to precipitate already seven States into insurrection a rebellion, because they are displeased with the results of a presidential election; or I could persuade myself, with the gentleman from Massachusetts, [Mr. ADAMS,] th thirteen States, or fifteen States, and eleven or twelve millions people have be already drawn or may soon be drawn into a revolt against the grandest and mo beneficent Government, in form and in practice, that ever existed, from no oth than the trivial and most frivolous causes which he has assigned, then I should i deed regard this revolution in the midst of which we are, as the most extraordina phenomenon ever recorded in history. But the muse of history will, I venture say, not so write it down upon the scroll which she still holds in her hand, in th grand old Hall of Representatives where, linked to time, solemnly and sadly sl numbers out yet the fleeting hours of this perishing Republic. No; believe m Representatives, the causes for these movements lie deeper and are of longer dura tion than all this. If not, then the malady needs no extreme medicine, no healin remedies, nothing, nothing. Time, patience, forbearance, quiet—these, these alon will restore the Union in a few months. But, sir, I have not so read the history this country, especially for the last fourteen years. The causes, I repeat, are to b found in the practical workings of the system, and are to be removed only b remedies which go down to the very root of the evil; not, indeed, by eradicatin the passions which give it birth and strength—for even religion fails to accomplis that impossible mission—but by checking or taking away the power with which thes passions are armed for their work of evil and mischief.

I find, then, sir, the first or remote cause which has led to the incipient dismem berment of the Union, in the infinite honors and emoluments, the immense, an continually increasing, power and patronage of the Federal Government. Ever admission of new States; every acquisition of new territory; every increase of wealth population, or resources of any kind; all moral, social, intellectual, or inventive de velopment—the press, the telegraph, the railroad, and the application of steam i every form; whatsoever there is of greatness at home, or of national honor an glory abroad—all, all has inured to the aggrandizement of this central Government Part of this, certainly, is the result of causes which no constitutional restriction, n party policy, and no statesmanship can control; but much of it, nevertheless, from infringements of the Constitution, and from usurpations, abuses, corruptions, and mal-administration of the Government. In the very beginning, as I have said, a fixed policy of strengthening the General Government, in every department, was inaugurated by the Federal party; and this led to the bitter and vehement struggle, in the very first decade of the system, between the Democratic-Republicans and the Federalists; between the advocates of power and the friends of liberty; those who leaned strongly towards the General Government and those who were for State rights and State sovereignty—the followers of Hamilton and the disciples of Jefferson—which ended, in 1801, in the overthrow of the Federal party, and the inauguration of the Democratic policy, which demanded a simple Government, a strict construction of the Constitution, no public debt, no protective tariff, no system of internal improvements, no national bank, hard money for the public dues, and economical expenditures; and this policy, after a long and violent contest for more than forty years—a contest marked with various fortune, and occasional defeat, and sometimes temporary departure by its own friends—at last became the established policy of the Government, and so continued until this pestilent sectional question of slavery obliterated old party divisions, and obscured and hid over, and covered up for a time—if, indeed, it has not removed utterly—some, at least, of the ancient landmarks of the Democratic party. And yet, in spite of the overthrow of the Federal party; in spite of the final defeat of its policy, looking especially and purposely to the strengthening of the General Government, partly from natural causes, as I have said, and partly because the Democratic party has sometimes been false to its professed principles—above all, to its great doctrine of State rights, and its true and wise policy of economy in expenditures, and decrease in executive patronage and influence—the Federal Government has gone on, steadily increasing in power and strength and honor and consideration and *corruption*, too, from the hour of its inauguration to this day; and when I speak of "corruption," I use the word in the sense in which British statesmen use it—men who understand the word, and who have, for a century and a half, reduced the thing itself to a science and a system, and have made it an element of very great strength in the British government.

Nor, sir, is this mischief, if mischief indeed it be, confined wholly to any one department of the General Government? The Federal judiciary—to begin with it—here and in the States, dazzles the imagination and invites the ambition of the lawyers, that not most numerous but yet most powerful class of citizens, by its superior honors, its great emoluments, its life tenure, its faith in precedents, and its settled forms and ancient practice, untouched by codes and unshaken by crude and reckless and hasty legislation. Here, in this venerable forum, where States at home and States and empires from abroad, and the Federal Government itself, are accustomed to contend for the judgment of the court, whatever there yet remains of ancient and black-letter law; whatever of veneration and regard for the names and memories, and the volumes of Littleton and Coke and Croke and Plowden, and the year books; or for silk gowns, and for all else, too, that is valuable in legal archæology, has taken refuge, and stands intrenched. All that there was of form and ceremony and dignity and decorum, in the beginning of the Government, is still to be found here, and only here; all but the bench and bar of forty years ago—the Marshalls and the Storys, the Harpers, the Pinckneys, the Wirts, and the Websters, of an age gone by.

Still, the circle of honor through the judiciary is a narrow one, and it lies open to but few; and yet, in times past, the judiciary has done much to enlarge the powers and increase the consideration and importance of the central Government.

But it is the Senate and the House of Representatives which are the great objects of ambition and the seats of power. All the legislative powers of this great and mighty Republic, whose name and authority and majesty are known and felt, and feared too, throughout the earth, are vested in the Congress of the United States. War, revenues, credit, disbursement, commerce, coinage, the postal system, the punishment of crimes upon the high seas and against the law of nations, the admission of new States, the disposition of the public lands, armies, navies, the militia, all belong to it to control, together with an unnumbered, innumerable, and most indefinable host of implied or derivative powers: whence funding systems, banks, protective tariffs, internal improvements, distributions, surveys, explorations, railroads, land grants, submarine telegraphs, postal steam navigation and post roads upon the high seas, plunder schemes, speculations and peculations, pensions, claims, the acquisition and government of Territories, and a long train of usurpations and abuses all tending—legitimate powers and illegitimate assumptions of power alike—to aggrandize the central Government, and to make its possession and control the highest object of a corrupt, wicked, perverted, and peculating ambition, in any party or any section.

But great and imposing as the powers, honors, and consideration of Congress are, the executive department is scarce inferior in anything, and in some things is far superior to it. Your President stands in the place of a king. There is a divinity that doth hedge him in; it is the divinity of PATRONAGE. He is the god whose priests are a hundred and fifty thousand, and whose worshipers a host whom no man can number; and the sacrifices of these priests and worshipers are literally "a broken spirit." Sir, your President is commander-in-chief of your armies, your navies, and of the militia—four millions of men. He carries on war, concludes peace, and makes treaties of every sort. Through his qualified veto, he is a participant in the entire legislation of the Government, and it behooves the whole army of speculators, jobbers, contractors, and claimants, to propitiate him as well as Senators and Representatives. He calls the Congress together on extraordinary occasions, and adjourns them in case of disagreement. He appoints and receives embassadors and all other diplomatic agents; appoints judges of the Supreme Court, and of other judicial tribunals; Cabinet ministers; collectors of customs, and postmasters; and controls the appointment of a hundred and fifty thousand other officers of every grade, from Secretary of State down to the humblest tide-waiter. All that is implied in the word "patronage," and all that is meant by that other word, the "spoils,"—*res detestabilis et caduca*—a word and a thing unknown to the fathers of the Republic, all belong to him to control. His power of appointment and removal at discretion makes him the master of every man who would look to the Executive for honor or emolument; and its tremendous influence is reflected back upon the Senate and this House, on every Senator or Representative who would reward his friends for their support at home, or secure new friends for a re-election. The Constitution forbids titles of nobility; yet your President is the founta of hon r. Sir, to pass by the utter and extraordinary perversion of the original pu pose of the Constitution in the choice of electors for the President—a perversion t result of caucuses, national conventions, and other party machinery, and which has l to those violent and debauching presidential struggles every four years for possessic of the immense spoils of the executive office—no department has, in other respec also, so utterly outstripped the estimate of the founders of the Government; excep indeed, of the few who, like Patrick Henry, were derided as ghost-seers and hypocho driacs.

When the elder Adams was President, the great east-room of the White House- where now, or lately, on gala days are gathered the embassadors and ministers of hundred courts, from Mexico to Japan, and the assembled wit, and fashion, an beauty, and distinction of the thirty-three States of the Union—was then used b the excellent and patriotic wife of the President as a drying-room for—not the maid of honor—but the washerwoman of the palace.

Sir, there is an incident connected with the early settlement of this city—still th capital of the Republic, selected as the seat of Government by Washington, th father of the Republic, and bearing his honored name—an incident which show how much he and the other great men who made the Constitution underestimate the power and importance of the Executive. This Capitol, within which we now deliberate, *fronts to the east.* There all your Presidents are inaugurated; and it wa the design and the expectation of the founders of the city that it should extend t the eastward. There, sir, there, in that direction, was to be the future Rome of the American continent. The Executive mansion was meant to be in the rear, and t be kept in the rear of the Chambers of the Legislature. A long vista through the original forest trees—a sort of American mall—was to connect them together; and the President was expected to enter below stairs and at the back door into this Capitol. But he was to be kept for the most part *trans Tiberem*—on the other side of the Tiber. The low, marshy ground to the westward, it was supposed, would forever forbid the building up of a city between the seats of legislative and executive magistracy; and the whole, if indeed ever laid out at all, might have become a great national park. But behold the strange perversity of man! The city has all gone to the westward. The rear of the Capitol has now become its front. Pennsylvania Avenue, instead of a suburban drive, is now a grand thoroughfare, the chief artery which conveys the blood from that which is now the center or heart of the system—the President. The Executive mansion—that old castle, with bad fires and without bells, to the sore discomfort of Mistress Abigail Adams—is now, and has been for years, the great object of attraction; and whereas, in the beginning, the "taverns"—for that was the name given them sixty years ago—all clustered around this Capitol, I observe that now the greatest, most flourishing, and best patronized "hotel" has established itself within bow-shot of the White House. Sir, the power of executive gravitation has proved too strong for the framers of the Government and the founders of the city. Westward the course of architecture has taken its way; and certainly, sir, certainly, it is not because of any especial attraction about that most venerable of ancient marts—old Georgetown.

But to resume, sir. Nothing adds so much to the power and influence of the Executive as a large revenue and heavy expenditures; and if a public debt be added, so much the worse. Every dollar more borrowed or collected, and every dollar more spent, is just so much added to the power and value of the executive office. Nothing in the political history of the country has been so marked as the steady, but enormous, increase in the taxation and disbursement of the Federal Government. Fifteen years ago—to go back no further—just previous to the Mexican war, the receipts of the Treasury were $29,000,000, and the expenditures $27,000,000; while four years ago, only ten years later, the receipts had run up to $69,000,000, and the expenditures to $71,000,000—the latter being always, or nearly always, a little in advance of the former. Nature, it is said, sir, abhors a vacuum; but government, our Government, at least, would seem to abhor a plethoric Treasury. There are always surgeons, volunteers, too, at that, if need be, of a very famous school of surgery, who are ready to resort upon all occasions to financial phlebotomy. Verily, sir, verily these surgeons of the executive household have great faith in a low fiscal regimen.

The collection and disbursement of $80,000,000 a year, for four years, is a prize worth every sacrifice. The power of the sword, the command of armies and navies and the militia, is itself a tremendous power; and from the signs around us, from all that everywhere meets the eye or falls upon the ear, at every step throughout this capital, I am afraid that now at length, and before the close of the last quarter of the first century of the Republic, it is about to assume a terrible significancy, and that the reign of military despotism is henceforth to be dated from this year. But great as this power is, it is nothing, nothing as yet in this country, compared with the power of the purse. He who commands that unnumbered host of eager and hungry expectants whose eyes are fixed upon the Treasury, to say nothing of that other host of seekers of office, is mightier far than the commander of military legions. The gentleman from Tennessee [Mr. ETHERIDGE] entertained us the other day with a glowing picture of the exodus of the present incumbents about the executive offices and elsewhere. Sir, I should be pleased, when he next addresses the House, to have his fine powers of wit and eloquence tested by a description of the flight of the incoming locusts about the fourth of March. Certainly, sir, certainly the departure of the army of fat, sleek, contented, well fed and well clad officeholders, whose natural *habitat* is the Treasury building, or some other of the same sort, is a picture melancholy enough to excite commiseration in even the hardest and the stoniest heart. But the ingress of that other mighty host of office seekers, fifty to one; lean, lank, cadaverous, hungry, hollow eyed; with bones bursting through their garments, and long, skinny fingers, eager to clutch the spoils; and stung, too, with the *œstrus* of that practical sort of patriotism which loves the country for its material benefits, would require some part at least of the powers of those diabolical old painters of the Spanish or Italian school. The gentleman will pardon me, but I am sure that even he is not equal to it.

Such, Mr. Speaker, is the central Government of the United States, and such its powers and honors and emoluments; and every year adds strength to them. Against the centralizing tendencies and influences of such a Government, the States separately cannot contend. Neither ambition nor avarice, the love of honor, or the love of gain, find anything to satisfy their large desires in the State governments. Sir, the State executives have no cabinets, no veto for the most part, no army, no navy, no militia, except upon the peace establishment, and that commonly despised; no foreign appointments, and no diplomatic intercourse; no treaties, no post office, no land office, no great revenues to disburse; small salaries, and no patronage—in short, sir, nothing to arouse ambition, or to excite avarice. The Legislatures of the States have a most valuable, but not the most dignified, field of labor. They declare no war, levy no imports, regulate no external commerce, coin no money, establish no post-routes, oceanic or overland; make no land grants, emit no bills of credit of their own, publish no Globe, have no franking privilege, and their senators and representatives serve the State for a few hundred dollars a year. The State judiciaries, however important the litigation before them may be to the parties, attract commonly but small interest from the public; and of late years, no great or splendid legal reputation is to be acquired outside of a few of the larger cities at least, either upon the bench or at the bar of the State courts. Whatever, sir, the dignity or power or consideration of the United States may be, that of each State is but the one thirty-fourth part of it; and, indeed, for some years past, the control of the State governments has, to a great extent, been sought after chiefly as an instrumentality for securing control of legislative, executive, or judicial position in the Federal Government. And all this mischief—for mischief certainly I must regard it—has been steadily aggravated by the policy pursued in nearly all the States, of diminishing in every way, in their constitutions, and by their laws, the dignity, power, and consideration of the several departments of their State governments. Short tenures, low salaries, biennial sessions, crude, hasty, and continually changing legislation, new constitutions every ten years, and whatever else may be classed under the head of reform, falsely so called, have been the bane of State sovereignty and importance. Indeed, for years past, State constitutions, laws, and institutions of every sort, seem to have been regarded as but so many subjects for rude and wanton experiment at the hands of reckless ideologists or demagogues. But besides all this, the infinite subdivision of political power in the States, from the chief departments of State down through counties, townships, school districts, cities, towns, and villages, all which certainly is very necessary and proper in a democratic Government, tends very much of itself to decrease the dignity and importance of the States. In short, sir, in nearly all the States, and especially in the new States, the great purpose of the politicians would seem to have been to ascertain just how feeble and simple and insignificant their governments could be made—just how near to a pure and perfect democracy our representative form of republicanism can be carried. All this, sir,

*

would have been well and consistent enough, no doubt, if the States were totally disconnected, or if the Federal Government could have been kept down equally low, simple, and democratic. Certainly, this is the true idea of a strictly democratic form and administration of government; and the nearer it is approached, the purer and better the system—in theory at least. But the experiment having been fairly tried, and the fact settled, that in a country so large, wealthy, populous, and enterprising as ours is, it is impossible to reduce down, or to keep down, the central Government to one of economy and simplicity; it is the true wisdom and policy of the States to see to it that their own separate governments are not rendered any more insignificant, at least, than they are already.

Such, sir, I repeat, then, is the central Government of the United States, and such its great and tremendous powers and honors and emoluments. With such powers, such honors, such patronage, and such revenues, is it any wonder, I ask, that everything, yes, even virtue, truth, justice, patriotism, and the Constitution itself, should be sacrificed to obtain possession of it? There is no such glittering prize to be contended for every four or two years, anywhere throughout the whole earth; and accordingly, from the beginning, and every year more and more, it has been the object of the highest and lowest, the purest and the most corrupt ambition known among men. Parties and combinations have existed from the first, and have been changed and reorganized, and built up and cast down, from the earliest period of our history to this day, all for the purpose of controlling the powers, and honors, and the moneys of the central Government. For a good many years parties were organized upon questions of finance or of political economy. Upon the subjects of a permanent public debt, a national bank, the public deposits, a protective tariff, internal improvements, the disposition of the public lands, and other questions of a similar character, all of them looking to the special interests of the moneyed classes, parties were for a long while divided. The different kinds of capitalists sometimes also disagreed among themselves—the manufacturers with the commercial men of the country; and in this manner party issues were occasionally made up. But the great dividing line at last, was always between capital and labor—between the few who had money and who wanted to use the Government to increase and "protect" it, as the phrase goes, and the many who had little but wanted to keep it, and who only asked Government to let them alone. Money, money, sir, was at the bottom of the political contests of the times; and nothing so curiously demonstrates the immense power of money as the fact that in a country where there is no entailment of estates, no law of primogeniture, no means of keeping up vast accumulations of wealth in particular families, no exclusive privileges, and where universal suffrage prevails, these contests should have continued, with various fortune, for full half a century. But at the last the opponents of Democracy, known at different periods of the struggle by many different names, but around whom the moneyed interests always rallied, were overborne and utterly dispersed. The Whig party, their last refuge, the last and ablest of the economic parties, died out; and the politicians who were not of the Democratic party, with a good many more, also, who had been of it, but who had deserted it, or whom it had deserted, were obliged to resort to some other and new element for an organization which might be made strong enough to conquer and to destroy the Democracy, and thus obtain control of the Federal Government. And most unfortunately for the peace of the country, and for the perpetuity, I fear, of the Union itself, they found the nucleus of such an organization ready formed to their hands—an organization odious, indeed, in name, but founded upon two of the most powerful passions of the human heart: SECTIONALISM, which is only a narrow and localized patriotism, and ANTI-SLAVERY, or love of freedom, which commonly is powerful just in proportion as it is very near coming home to one's own self, or very far off, so that either self-interest or the imagination can have full power to act.

And here let me remark, that it had so happened that almost, if not quite, from the beginning of the Government, the South, or slaveholding section of the Union—partly because the people of the South are chiefly an agricultural and producing, a non-commercial and non-manufacturing people, and partly because there is no conflict, or little conflict, among them between labor and capital, inasmuch as to a considerable extent capital owns a large class of their laborers not of the white race; and it may be also because, as Mr. Burke said many years ago, the holders of slaves are "by far the most proud and jealous of their freedom," and because the aristocracy of birth and family, and of talent, is more highly esteemed among them than the aristocracy of wealth—but no matter from what cause, the fact was that the South for fifty years was nearly always on the side of the Democratic party. It was the natural ally of the Democracy of the North, and especially of the West. Geographical position and identity of interests bound us together; and till this sectional question of slavery arose, the South and the new States of the West were always together; and the latter, in the beginning at least, always Democratic. Sir, there was not a triumph of the Democratic party in half a century which was not won by the aid of the statesmen and the people of the South. I would not be understood, however, as intimating that the South was ever slow to appropriate her full share of the spoils—the *opima spolia* of victory, or especially that the politicians of that great and noble old Commonwealth of Virginia—God bless her—were ever remarkable for the grace of self-denial in this regard—not at all. But it was natural, sir, that they who had been so many times, and for so many years, baffled and defeated by the aid of the South, should entertain no very kindly feelings towards her. And here I must not omit to say, that all this time there was a powerful minority in the whole South, sometimes a majority in the whole South, and always in some of the States of the South, who belonged to the several parties which, at different times, contended with the Democracy for the possession and control of the Federal Government. Parties in those days were not sectional, but extended into every State and every part of the Union. And, indeed, in the convention of 1787, the possibility, or at least the probability, of sectional combinations seems, as I have already said, to have been almost wholly overlooked. Washington, it is true, in his Farewell Address warned us against them, but it was rather as a distant vision than as a near reality; and a few years later, Mr. Jefferson speaks of a possibility of the people of the Mississippi valley seceding from the East; for even then a division of the Union, North and South, or by slave lines, in the Union or out of it, seems scarcely to have been contemplated. The letter of Mr. Jefferson upon this subject, dated in 1803, is a curious one; and I commend it to the attention of gentlemen upon both sides of the House.

So long, sir, as the South maintained its equality in the Senate, and something like equality in population, strength, and material resources in the country, there was little to invite aggression, while there were the means, also, to repel it. But, in the course of time, the South lost its equality in the other wing of the Capitol, and every year the disparity between the two sections became greater and greater. Meantime, too, the anti-slavery sentiment, which had lain dormant at the North for many years after the inauguration of the Federal Government, began, just about the time of the emancipation in the British West Indies, to develop itself in great strength, and with wonderful rapidity. It had appeared, indeed, with much violence at the period of the admission of Missouri, and even then shook the Union to its foundation. And yet how little a sectional controversy, based upon such a question, had been foreseen by the founders of the Government, may be learned from Mr. Jefferson's letter to Mr. Holmes, in 1820, where he speaks of it falling upon his ear like "a fire bell in the night." Said he:

"I considered it, at once, as the death knell of the Union. It is hushed, indeed, for the moment; but this is a reprieve only, not a final sentence. A geographical line, *coinciding with a marked principle, moral and political*,"—

Sir, it is this very coincidence of geographical line with the marked principle, moral and political, of slavery, which I propose to reach and to obliterate in the only way possible; by running other lines, coinciding with other and less dangerous principles, none of them moral, and, above all, with other and conflicting interests—

"A geographical line coinciding with a marked principle, moral and political, 'once conceived and held up to the angry passions of men, will never be obliterated, 'and every new irritation will mark it deeper and deeper." * * * * * * * * * * "I regret that I am now to die in the belief that 'the useless sacrifice of themselves by the generation of 1776, to acquire self-govern-'ment and happiness to their country, is to be thrown away by the unwise and 'unworthy passions of their sons; and that my only consolation is to be that I shall 'not live to weep over it."

Fortunate man! He did not live to weep over it. To-day he sleeps quietly beneath the soil of his own Monticello, unconscious that the mighty fabric of Government which he helped to rear—a Government whose foundations were laid by the hands of so many patriots and sages, and cemented by the blood of so many martyrs and heroes—hastens now, day by day, to its fall. What recks he, or that other great man, his compeer, fortunate in life and opportune alike in death, whose dust they keep at Quincy, of those dreadful notes of preparation in every State for civil strife and fraternal carnage; or of that martial array which already has changed this once peaceful capital into a beleagured city? Fortunate men! They died while the Constitution yet survived, while the Union survived, while the spirit of fraternal affection still lived, and the love of true American liberty lingered yet in the hearts of their descendants.

Sir, the antagonism of parties founded on money or questions of political economy having died out, and the balance of power between the North and the South being now lost, and the strength and dignity, and the revenues and disbursements—the patronage and spoils—of the Federal Government having grown to an enormous size, was anything more natural than the organization, *upon any basis peculiar to the stronger section*, of a sectional party, to secure so splendid and tempting a prize? Or was anything more inevitable, than that the "marked principle, moral and political," of slavery, *coinciding with the very geographical line which divided the two sections*, and appealing so strongly to northern sentiments and prejudices, and against which it was impossible for any man or any party long to contend, should be revived? Unhappily, too, just about this time, the acquisition of a very large territory from Mexico, not foreseen or provided for by the Missouri compromise, opened wide the door for this very question of slavery, in a form every way the most favorable to the agitators. The Wilmot proviso, or congressional prohibition—now indeed exploded, but which, nevertheless received, in some form or other, the indorsement of every free State then in the Union—it was proposed to establish over the whole territory thus acquired, as well south of 36° 30′ as north of that lattitude. The proposition, upon the other hand, to extend the Missouri compromise line to the Pacific, was rejected by the votes of almost the entire Whig party, and of a large majority, I believe, of the Democratic party of the free States. That, sir, was the fatal mistake of the North; and in tribulation and anguish will she and the other sections of the Union, and our posterity, too, for ages, it may be, weep tears of bloody repentance and regret over it.

This controversy, however, sir, after having again shaken the Union to its center, was at last, though with great difficulty, adjusted through the compromise measures of 1850, by the last of the great statesmen of the second period of the Republic. But four years afterwards, upon the bill to organize the Territories of Kansas and Nebraska, upon the principles of the legislation of 1850, the imprisoned winds—Eurus, Notusque, *creberque procellis Africus*—were all again let loose with more than the rage of a tropical hurricane. The Missouri restriction, which for years had been denounced as a wicked and atrocious concession to slavery, and which, some thirty years before, had consigned almost every free State Senator or Representative who supported it to political oblivion, became now a most sacred compact which it was sacrilege to touch. A distinguished Senator, late the Governor of Ohio, who had entitled his great speech against the adjustment measures of 1850, "*Union and Freedom without Compromise*," now put forth his elaborate defense, four years later, of the Missouri restriction, with the rubric or text, in ambitious characters, "*Maintain Plighted Faith.*" But, right or wrong, wise or unwise, at the time, as the repeal of that restriction may have seemed, subsequent acts and events have made it both a delusion and a snare. Yes, sir, I confess it. I who, as a private citizen, was one of its earliest defenders, make open confession of it here, to-day. It was this which gave a new and terrible vitality, to the languishing element of abolitionism, and which precipitated, at least, a crisis which, I fear, was nevertheless, sooner or later, inevitable. It is the crisis of which the President elect spoke three years ago. It is, indeed, reached. Would to God it were passed, also, in peace.

But, sir, whether the leaders of the movement against the repeal of the Missouri restriction were consistent or inconsistent, honest or dishonest, the great mass of the people of the free States were roused for a time to the highest indignation by it; and inasmuch as the Whig party was just then falling to pieces, wicked, or reckless, or short-sighted men, eagerly seized upon this unsettled condition of the public mind, to reorganize the Free-Soil party of 1848, under a new and captivating name, but very nearly upon the principles of the Buffalo platform of that year; thus abandoning the extreme abolition sentiments of the Liberty party, and bringing up the great majority of the Whig party, and not a few of the Democratic party also, to the Free-Soil and non-slavery extension principle; and by this compromise, forming and consolidating that powerful party, which, for the first time in our history, by a mere sectional plurality —in a minority in fact by a million of votes—has obtained possession of the power and patronage of the central Government. Sir, if all this had happened solely by accident, and were likely never to be repeated, portentous as it might be of present evil, it would have caused, and ought to have caused, none of the disasters which have already followed. But the DREAD SECRET once disclosed, that the immense powers and revenues and honors and spoils, of this great and mighty Republic, may be easily won, by a mere sectional majority, upon a popular sectional issue, will never die; and new aggressions and new issues must continually spring from it. This is the philosophy and the justification of the alarm and consternation which have shaken the South from the Potomac to the Gulf. It is the philosophy and the justification, too, of the amendment of the gentleman from Massachusetts, [MR. ADAMS,] and of all the other propositions for new adjustments and new guarantees. Sir, the gentleman from New York, [MR. SEDGWICK,] was right when he said that there never was any great event which did not spring from some adequate cause. The South is afraid of your sectional majority, organized and consolidated upon the abstract principle of hostility to slavery generally, and the practical application of that principle to the exclusion of slavery from all the Territories, and its restriction by the power of that sectional majority, to where it now exists. And if this be not the fundamental doctrine of the Republican party, I shall be greatly obliged to some gentleman of that party to tell me what its fundamental doctrine is.

But unjust and oppressive as the South feel their exclusion from the common territories of the States to be, they know well, also, that the propelling power of a great moral and religious principle, as it is regarded in the North, added to the still more enduring, persistent, and prudent passion of ambition, of thirst for power and place, for the honors and emoluments of such a Government as ours, with its half a million of dependents and expectants, and its eighty millions of revenues and disbursements, all, all to be secured by the Aladdin's lamp of a sectional majority, cannot be arrested or extinguished by anything short of the suppression of the power which makes it potent for mischief. And nothing less than this, be assured, will satisfy any considerable number of even the more moderate of the people of the border slave States, and certainly without it there is not the slightest hope of the return of the States upon the Gulf, and thus of a restoration of the Union as it existed but three months ago. The statesmen and the people of all of these States well know, also, that by the civil law of every country among individuals, and by the law of nations, as between sovereign and foreign States, the power to aggress, along with the threat and the preparation to aggress, is a good cause why an individual or a State should be required to give some adequate assurance that the power shall not be used to execute the threat; or, otherwise, that the power shall itself be taken away. Apply now, sir, these principles to the case in hand. The North has the power; that power is in the hands of the Republican party, and already, they have resolved to use it for the exclusion of the South from all the Territories. There shall be no more extension of slavery. More than this, the leaders of the party—many of them leaders and founders of the old Liberty Guard, the original Abolition party of the North—the very men who brought the masses of the Whig party and many of the Democratic party from utter indifference and non-intervention, years ago, upon the question of slavery up to the point of no more slavery extension, and persuaded them, in spite of the warning voice of Washington, in the very face of the appalling danger of disunion, to unite for this purpose, in a powerful sectional party, for the first time in the history of the Government—these self-same leaders proclaim now, not indeed as present doctrines or purposes of the Republican party; but as solemn abstract truths, as fixed, existing facts, that there is a "higher law" than the Constitution, and an "irrepressible conflict" of principle and interest between the dominant and the minority sections of the Union; and that one or the other must conquer in the conflict. Sir, in this contest with ballots, who is it that must conquer—the section of the minority or the section of the majority?

And now, sir, when sentiments like these are held and proclaimed—deliberately, solemnly, repeatedly proclaimed—by men, one of whom is now the President elect, and the other the Secretary of State of the incoming Administration, is it at all surprising that the States of the South should be filled with excitement and alarm, or that they should demand, as almost with one voice they have demanded, adequate and complete guarantees for their rights and security against aggression? Right or wrong, justifiably or without cause, they have done it: and I lament to say that some of the States have even gone so far as to throw off wholly the authority of the Federal Government, and withdraw themselves from the Union. Sir, I will not discuss the right of secession. It is of no possible avail, now, either to maintain or to condemn it: yet it is vain to tell me that States *cannot* secede. Seven States *have* seceded; they now refuse any longer to recognize the authority of this Government, and already have entered into a new confederacy and set up a provisional government of their own. In three months their agents and commissioners will return from Europe with the recognition of Great Britain and France and of the other great Powers of the continent. Other States at home are preparing to unite with this new confederacy, if you do not grant to them their just and equitable demands. The question is no longer one of mere preservation of the Union. That was the question when we met in this Chamber some two months ago. Unhappily, that day has passed by; and while your "perilous committee of thirty-three" debated and deliberated to gain time—yes, to gain time—for that was the insane and most unstatesmanlike cry in the beginning of the session, star after star shot madly from our political firmament. The question to-day is: how shall we now keep the States we have and restore those which are lost? Ay, sir, *restore*, till every wanderer shall have returned, and not one be missing from the "starry flock."

If, then, Mr. Speaker, I have justly and truly stated the causes which have led to these most disastrous results; if indeed the control of the immense powers, honors, and revenues—the spoils—of the Federal Government; in a word, if the possession of power and the temptation to abuse it be the primary cause of the present dismemberment of the United States, ought not every remedy proposed to reach at once the very seat of the disease? And why, sir, may not the malady be healed? Why cannot this controversy be adjusted? Has, indeed, the Union of these States received the immedicable wound? I do not believe it. Never was there a political crisis for which wise, courageous, and disinterested statesmen could more speedily devise a remedy. British statesmen would have adjusted it in a few weeks. Twice certainly, if not three times, in this century, they have healed troubles threatening a dissolution of the monarchy and civil war; and each time healed them by yielding promptly to the necessities which pressed upon them, giving up principles and measures to which they had every way for years been committed. They have learned wisdom from the obstinacy of the King who lost to Great Britain her thirteen colonies, and have been taught by that memorable lesson to concede and to compromise in time, and to do it radically; and history has pronounced it statesmanship, not weakness. In each case, too, they yielded up, not doctrines and a policy which they were seeking for the first time to establish, but the ancient and settled principles, usages, and institutions of the realm; and they yielded up these to save others yet more essential, and to maintain the integrity of the empire. They did save it, and did maintain it; and to-day Great Britain is stronger and more prosperous and more secure than any Government on the globe.

Sir, no man had for a longer time, or with more inexorable firmness, opposed Catholic emancipation than the Duke of Wellington. Yet, when the issue came at last between emancipation or civil war, the hero of a hundred battle-fields, the conqueror at Waterloo, the greatest military commander, except Napoleon, of modern times; yes, the IRON DUKE, lost not a moment, but yielded to the storm, and himself led the party which carried the great measure of peace and compromise through the very citadel of conservatism—the House of Lords. Sir, he sought no middle ground, no half-way measure, confessing weakness, promising something, doing nothing. And in that memorable debate he spoke words of wisdom, moderation, and true courage, which I commend to gentlemen in this House; to our Wellington outside of it, and to all others anywhere, whose parched jaws seem ravenous for blood. He said:

"It has been my fortune to have seen much of war—more than most men. I have 'been constantly engaged in the active duties of the military profession from boyhood 'until I have grown gray. My life has been passed in familiarity with scenes of death 'and human suffering. Circumstances have placed me in countries where the 'war was internal—between opposite parties in the same nation; and rather than a 'country I loved should be visited with the calamities which I have seen, *with the 'unutterable horrors of civil war, I would run any risk; I would make any sacrifice; 'I would freely lay down my life.* There is nothing which destroys property and 'prosperity, and demoralizes character, to the extent which civil war does. By it, 'the hand of man is raised against his neighbor, against his brother, and against his 'father; the servant betrays his master, and the master ruins his servant. *Yet this is 'the resource to which we must have looked, these are the means which we must have applied, in order to have put an end to this state of things, if we had not embraced the 'option of bringing forward the measure for which I hold myself responsible.*"

Two years later, sir, in a yet more dangerous crisis upon the Reform Bill, which the Commons had rejected, and when civil commotion and discord, if not revolution, were again threatened, and it became necessary to dissolve the Parliament, and for that purpose to secure the consent of a King adverse to the dissolution, the Lord Chancellor of England, one of the most extraordinary men of the age, by perhaps the boldest and most hazardous experiment ever tried upon royalty, surprised the King into consent, assuring him that the further existence of the Parliament was incompatible with the peace and safety of the kingdom; and having, without the royal command, summoned the great officers of State, prepared the crown, the robes, the King's speech, and whatever else was needed, and, at the risk of the penalties of high treason, ordered also the attendance of the troops required by the usages of the ceremony, he hurried the King to the Chamber of the House of Lords, where, in the presence of the Commons, the Parliament was dissolved, while each House was still in high debate, and without other notice in advance than the sound of the cannon which announced his Majesty's approach. Yet all this was done in the midst of threatened insurrection and rebellion; when the Duke of Wellington, the Duke of Cumberland, and other noblemen, were assaulted in the streets, and their houses broken into and mobbed; when London itself was threatened with capture, and the dying Sir Walter Scott was hooted and reviled by ruffians at the polls. It was done while the kingdom was one vast mob; while the cry rang through all England, Ireland, and Scotland, that the bill must be carried *through* Parliament or *over* Parliament; if possible, by peaceable means; if not possible, then by force; and when the Prime Minister declared in the House of Commons that, by reason of its defeat, "much blood would be shed in the struggle between the contending parties, and that he was perfectly convinced that the British Constitution would perish in the conflict." And, sir, when all else failed, the King himself at last gave permission in writing, to Earl Grey and the Lord Chancellor, to create as many new peers as might be necessary to secure a majority for the reform bill in the House of Lords.

Such, sir, is British statesmanship. They remember, but we have forgotten, the lessons which our fathers taught them. Sir, it will be the opprobrium of American statesmanship forever that this controversy of ours shall be permitted to end in final and perpetual dismemberment of the Union.

I propose now, sir, to consider briefly the several propositions before the House, looking to the adjustment of our difficulties by constitutional amendment, in connection also with those which I have myself had the honor to submit.

Philosophically or logically considered, there are two ways in which the work before us may be effected: the first, by removing the temptation to aggress; the second, by taking the power away. Now, sir, I am free to confess that I do not see how any amendment of the Constitution can diminish the powers, dignity, or patronage of the Federal Government, consistently with the just distribution of power between the several departments; or between the States and the General Government, consistently with its necessary strength and efficiency. The evil here lies rather in the administration than in the organization of the system; and a large part of it is inherent in the administration of every government. The virtue and intelligence of the people, and the capacity and honesty of their representatives in every department, must be intrusted with the mitigation and correction of the mischief. The less the legislation of every kind, the smaller the revenues, and fewer the disbursements; the less the Government shall have to do, every way, with debt, credit, moneyed influences, and jobs and schemes of every sort, the longer peace can be maintained; and the more the number of the employees and dependents on Government can be reduced, the less will be the patronage and the corruption of the system, and the less, therefore, the motive to sacrifice truth and justice, and to overleap the Constitution to secure the control of it. In other words, the more you diminish temptation, the more you will deliver us from evil.

But I pass this point by without further remark, inasmuch as none of the plans of adjustment proposed, either here or in the Senate, look to any change of the Constitution in this respect. They all aim—every one of them—at checking the POWER to aggress; and, except the amendment of the gentleman from Massachusetts, [Mr. ADAMS,] which goes much further than mine in giving a negative upon one subject to every slave State in the Union, they propose to effect their purpose by mere constitutional prohibitions. It is not my purpose, sir, to demand a vote upon the propositions which I have myself submitted. I have not the party position, nor the power behind me, nor with me, nor the age, nor the experience which would justify me in assuming the lead in any great measure of peace and conciliation; but I believe, and very respectfully I suggest it, that something similar, at least, to these propositions will form a part of any adequate and final adjustment which may restore all the States to the Federal Union. No, sir; I am able now only to follow where others may lead.

I shall vote for the amendment of the gentleman from Massachusetts, [Mr. Adams,] (though it does not go far enough,) because it ignores and denies the moral or religious element of the anti-slavery agitation, and thus removes so far, at least, its most dangerous sting—*fanaticism*—and dealing with the question as one of mere policy and economy, of pure politics alone, proposes a new and most comprehensive guarantee for the peculiar institution of the States of the South. I shall vote also for the Crittenden propositions—as an experiment, and only as an experiment—because they proceed upon the same general idea which marks the Adams amendment; and whereas, for the sake of peace and the Union, the latter would give a new security to slavery in the States, the former, for the self-same great and paramount object of Union and peace, proposes to give a new security also to slavery in the Territories south of the latitude 36° 30'. If the Union is worth the price which the gentleman from Massachusetts volunteers to pay to maintain it, is it not richly worth the very small additional price which the Senator from Kentucky demands as the possible condition of preserving it? Sir, it is the old parable of the Roman sybil; and to-morrow she will return with fewer volumes, and it may be at a higher price.

I shall vote to try the Crittenden propositions, because, also, I believe that they are perhaps the least which even the more moderate of the slave States would under any circumstances be willing to accept; and because north, south, and west, the people seem to have taken hold of them and to demand them of us, as an experiment at least. I am ready to try, also, if need be, the propositions of the border State committee, or of the peace congress; or any other fair, honorable, and reasonable terms of adjustment which may so much as promise even, to heal our present troubles, and to restore the Union of these States. Sir, I am ready and willing and anxious to try all things and to do all things "which may become a man," to secure that great object which is nearest to my heart.

But, judging all of these propositions, nevertheless, by the lights of philosophy and statesmanship, and as I believe they will be regarded by the historian who shall come after us, I find in them all two capital defects which will, in the end, prove them to be both unsatisfactory to large numbers alike of the people of the free and the slave States, and wholly inadequate to the great purpose of the reconstruction and future preservation of the Union. None of them—except that of the gentleman from Massachusetts, [Mr. Adams,] and his in one particular only—proposes to give to the minority section any veto or self-protecting power against those aggressions, the temptation to which, and the danger from which, are the very cause or reason for the demand for any new guarantees at all. They who complain of violated faith in the past, are met only with new promises of good faith for the future; they who tell you that you have broken the Constitution heretofore, are answered with proposed additions to the Constitution, so that there may be more room for breaches hereafter. The only protection here offered against the aggressive spirit of the majority, is the simple pledge of power that it will not abuse itself; nor aggress, nor usurp, nor amplify itself to attain its ends. You place in the distance, the highest honors, the largest emoluments, the most glittering of all prizes; and then you propose, as it were, to exact a promise from the race horse that he will accommodate his speed to the slow-moving pace of the tortoise. Sir, if I meant terms of equality, I would give the tortoise a good ways the start in the race.

My point of objection, therefore, is, that you do not allow to that very minority which, because it is a minority, and because it is afraid of your aggressions, is now about to secede and withdraw itself from your Government, and set up a separate confederacy of its own, you do not allow to it the power of self-protection within the Union. If, Representatives, you are sincere in your protestations that you do not mean to aggress upon the rights of this minority, you deny yourselves nothing by these new guarantees. If you do mean to aggress, then this minority has a right to demand self-protection and security.

But, sir, there remains yet another, and a still stronger objection to these several propositions. Every one of them proposes to recognize, and to embody in the Constitution, that very sort of sectionalism which is the immediate instrumentality of the present dismemberment of these States, and the existence of which is, in my judgment, utterly inconsistent with the peace and stability of the Union. Every one of them recognizes and perpetuates the division line between slave labor and free labor, that self-same "*geographical line, coinciding with the marked principle, moral and political*," of slavery, which so startled the prophetic ear of Jefferson, and which he foretold, forty years ago, every irritation would mark deeper and deeper, till, at last, it would destroy the Union itself. They one and all recognize slavery as an existing and paramount element in the politics of the country, and yet only promise that the non-slaveholding majority section, immensely in the majority, will not aggress upon the rights or trespass upon the interests of the slaveholding minority section, immensely in the minority. *Adeo senuerunt Jupiter et Mars?*

Sir, just so long as slavery is recognized as an element in politics at all—just so long as the dividing line between the slave labor and the free labor States is kept up as the only line, with the disparity between them growing every day greater and greater—just so long it will be impossible to keep the peace and maintain a Federal Union between them. However sufficient any of these plans of adjustment might have been one year ago, or even in December last when proposed, and prior to the secession of any of the States, I fear that they will be found utterly inadequate to restore the Union now. I do not believe that alone they will avail to bring back the States which have seceded, and therefore to withhold the other slave States from ultimate secession; for surely no man fit to be a statesman can fail to foresee that unless the cotton States can be returned to the Union, the border States must and will, sooner or later, follow them out of it. As between two confederacies—the one non-slaveholding, and the other slaveholding—all the States of the South must belong to the latter, except possibly Maryland and Delaware, and they of course could remain with the former only upon the understanding that just as soon as practicable slavery should be abolished within their limits. If fifteen slave States cannot protect themselves, and feel secure in a Union with eighteen anti-slavery States, how can eight slave States maintain their position and their rights in a Union with nineteen, or with thirty, anti-slavery States? The question, therefore, is not merely what will keep Virginia in the Union, but also what will bring Georgia back. And here let me say that I do not doubt that there is a large and powerful Union sentiment still surviving in all the States which have seceded, South Carolina alone perhaps excepted; and that if the people of those States can be assured that they shall have the power to protect themselves by their own action *within the Union*, they will gladly return to it, very greatly preferring protection within to security outside of it. Just now, indeed, the fear of danger, and your persistent and obstinate refusal to enable them to guard agaiast it, have delivered the people of those States over into the hands and under the control of the real secessionists and disunionists among them; but give them security and the means of enforcing it; above all, dry up this pestilent fountain of slavery agitation as a political element in both sections, and, my word for it, the ties of a common ancestry, a common kindred, and common language; the bonds of a common interest, common danger, and common safety; the recollections of the past, and of associations not yet dissolved, and the bright hopes of a future to all of us, more glorious and resplendent than any other country ever saw; ay, sir, and visions, too, of that old flag of the Union, and of the music of the Union, and precious memories of the statesmen and heroes of the dark days of the Revolution, will fill their souls yet again with desires and yearnings intense for the glories, the honors, and the material benefits, too, of that Union which their fathers and our fathers made; and they will return to it, not as the prodigal, but with songs and rejoicing, as the Hebrews returned from the captivity to the ancient city of their kings.

Proceeding, sir, upon the principles which I have already considered, and applying them to the causes which, step by step, have led to our present troubles, I have ventured with great deference to submit the propositions which are upon the table of the House. While not inconsistent with any of the other pending plans of adjustment, they are, in my judgment, and again I speak it with becoming deference, fully adequate to secure that protection from aggression, without which there can be no confidence, and therefore no peace and no restoration for the Union.

There are two maxims, sir, applicable to all constitutional reform, both of which it has been my purpose to follow. In the first place, not to amend more or further than is necessary for the mischief to be remedied; and next, to follow strictly the principles of the Constitution, which is to be amended; and corollary to these I might add that, in framing amendments, the words and phrases of the Constitution ought so far as practicable to be adopted.

I propose, then, sir, to do as all others in the Senate and the House have done, so far—to recognize the existence of sections as a fixed fact, which, lamentable as it is, can no longer be denied or suppressed; but, for the reasons I have already stated, I propose to establish four instead of two grand sections of the Union, all of them well known or easily designated by marked, natural, or geographical lines and boundaries. I propose four sections instead of two; because, if two only are recognized, the natural and inevitable division will be into slaveholding and non-slaveholding sections; and it is this very division, either by constitutional enactment, or by common consent, as hitherto, which, in my deliberate judgment and deepest conviction, it concerns the peace and stability of the Union should be forever hereafter ignored. Till then there cannot be, and will not be, perfect union and peace between these United States; because, in the first place, the nature of the question is such that it stirs up, necessarily, as forty years of strife conclusively proves, the strongest and the bitterest passions and antagonism possible among men; and, in the next place, because the non-slaveholding section has now, and will have to the end, a steadily increasing majority, and enormously disproportioned weight and influence in the Government; thus combining that which never can be very long resisted in any Government—the temptation and the power to aggress.

Sir, it was not the mere geographical line which so startled Mr. Jefferson in 1820; but the coincidence of that line with the marked principle, moral and political, of slavery. And now, sir, to remove this very mischief which he predicted, and which has already happened, it is essential that this coincidence should be obliterated; and the repeated failure, for years past, of all other compromises based upon a recognition of this coincidence, has proved beyond doubt that it cannot be obliterated unless it be by other and conflicting lines of principle and interests. I propose, therefore, to multiply the sections, and thus efface the slave-labor and free-labor division, and at the same time, and in this manner, to diminish the relative power of each section. And to prevent combinations among these different sections, I propose, also, to allow a vote in the Senate by sections, upon demand of one-third of the Senators of any section, and to require the concurrence of a majority of the Senators of each section in the passage of any measure in which, by the Constitution, it is necessary that the House, and therefore, also, the President, should concur. All this, sir, is perfectly consistent with the principles of the Constitution, as shown in the division of the legislative department into the two Houses of Congress; the veto power; the two-thirds vote of both Houses necessary to pass a bill over the veto; the provisions in regard to the ratification of treaties and amendments of the Constitution; but especially in the equal representation and suffrage of each State in the Senate, whereby the vote of Delaware, with a hundred thousand inhabitants, *vetoes* the vote of New York, with her population of nearly four millions. If the protection of the smaller States against the possible aggressions of the larger States required, in the judgment of the framers of the Constitution, this peculiar and apparently inequitable provision, why shall not the protection, by a similar power of veto, of the smaller and weaker sections against the aggressions of the larger and stronger sections, not be now allowed, when time and experience have proved the necessity of just such a check upon the majority? Does any one doubt that, if the men who made the Constitution had foreseen that the real danger to the system lay not in aggression by the large upon the small States, but in geographical combinations of the strong sections against the weak, they would have guarded jealously against that mischief, just as they did against the danger to which they mistakenly believed the Government to be exposed? And if this protection, sir, be now demanded by the minority as the price of the Union, so just and reasonable a provision ought not for a moment to be denied. Far better this than secession and disruption. This would, indeed, enable the minority to fight for their rights in the Union, instead of breaking it in pieces to secure them outside of it.

Certainly, sir, it is in the nature of a veto power to each section in the Senate; but necessity requires it, secession demands it, just as twice in the history of the Roman Commonwealth secession demanded and received the power of the tribunitian veto as he price of a restoration of the Republic. The secession to the Sacred Mount secured, just as a second secession half a century later restored, the veto of the tribunes of the people, and reinvigorated and preserved the Roman constitution for three hundred years. Vetoes, checks, balances, concurrent majorities—these, sir, are the true conservators of free Government.

But it is not in legislation alone that the danger or the temptation to aggress is to be found. Of the tremendous power and influence of the Executive I have already spoken. And, indeed, the present revolutionary movements are the result of the apprehension of executive usurpation and encroachments to the injury of the rights of the South. But for secession because of this apprehended danger, the legislative department would have remained, for the present at least, in other and safer hands. Hence the necessity for equal protection and guarantee against sectional combinations and majorities to secure the election of the President, and to control him when elected. I propose, therefore, that a concurrent majority of the electors, or States, or Senators, as the case may require, of each section, shall be necessary to the choice of President and Vice President; and lest, by reason of this increased complexity, there may be a failure of choice oftener than heretofore, I propose also a special election in such case, and an extension of the term in all cases to six years. This is the outline of the plan; the details may be learned in full from the joint resolution itself; and I will not detain the House by any further explanation now.

Sir, the natural and inevitable result of these amendments, will be to preclude the possibility of sectional parties and combinations to obtain possession of either the legislative or the executive power and patronage of the Federal Government; and, if not to suppress totally, at least, very greatly to diminish the evil results of national caucuses, conventions, and other similar party appliances. It will no longer be possible to elect a President by the votes of a mere dominant and majority section. Sectional issues must cease, as the basis at least of large party organizations. Ambition, or lust for power and place, must look no longer to its own section, but to the whole country; and he who would be President, or in any way the foremost among his countrymen, must consult, henceforth, the combined good and the good will, too, of all the sections, and in this way, consistently with the Constitution, can the "general welfare" be best attained. Thus, indeed, will the result be, instead of a narrow, illiberal, and sectional policy, an enlarged patriotism and extended public spirit.

If it be urged that the plan is too complex, and therefore impracticable, I answer that that was the objection in the beginning to the whole Federal system, and to almost every part of it. It is the argument of the French Republicans against the division of the legislative department into two Chambers; and it was the argument especially urged at first against the entire plan or idea of the electoral colleges for the choice of a President. But, if complex, I answer again, It will prevent more evil than good. If it suspend some legislation for a time, I answer, The world is governed too much. If it cause delay sometimes in both legislation and the choice of President, I answer yet again, Better, far better, this than disunion and the ten thousand complexities, peaceful and belligerent, which must attend it. Better, infinitely better this, in the Union, than separate confederacies outside of it, with either perpetual war or entangling and complicated alliances, offensive and defensive, from henceforth forever. To the South I say, If you are afraid of free State aggressions by Congress or the Executive, here is abundant protection for even the most timid. To the Republican party of the North and West I say, If you really tremble, as for years past you would have had us believe, over that terrible, but somewhat mythical, monster—the SLAVE POWER—here, too, is the utmost security for you against the possibility of its aggressions. And from first to last, allow me to say that, being wholly negative in its provisions, this plan can only prevent evil, and not work any positive evil itself. It is a shield for defense; not a sword for aggression. In one word, let me add that the whole purpose and idea of this plan of adjustment which I propose, is to give to the several sections *inside* of the Union that power of self-protection which they are resolved, or will some day or other be resolved, to secure for themselves *outside* of the Union.

I propose further, sir, that neither Congress, nor a Territorial Legislature shall have power to interfere with the equal right of migration, from all sections, into the Terrritories of the United States; and that neither shall have power to destroy or impair any rights of either person or property, in these Territories; and, finally, that new States, either when annexed or when formed out of any of the Territories, with the consent of Congress, shall be admitted into the Union, with any constitution, republican in form, which the people of such States may ordain.

And now, gentlemen of the South, why cannot you accept it? The Federal Government has never yet, in any way, aggressed upon your rights. Hitherto, indeed, it has been in your own, or at least in friendly hands. You only fear—being in the minority—that it will aggress, because it has now fallen under the control of those, who, you believe, have the temptation, the will, and the power to aggress. But this plan of adjustment proposes to take away the power; and of what avail will the temptation or the will then be, without the power to execute? Both must soon perish.

And why cannot you, of the Republican party, accept it? There is not a word about slavery in it, from beginning to end: I mean in the amendments. It is silent upon the question. South of 36° 30', and east of the Rio Grande, there is scarce any territory which is not now within the limits of some existing State; and west of that river, and of the Rocky Mountains, as well as north of 36° 30' and east of those mountains, though any new State should establish slavery, still her vote would be counted in the Senate and in the electoral colleges with the non-slaveholding section to which she would belong; just as if, within the limits of the South, any State should abolish slavery, or any new State not tolerating slavery should be admitted, the vote of such State would also be cast with the section of the South. However slavery might be extended, as a mere form of civilization or of labor, there could be no extension of it as a mere aggressive political element in the Government. If the South only demand that the Federal Government shall not be used aggressively to prohibit the extension of slavery; if she does not desire to use it herself, upon the other hand, positively to extend the institution, then she may well be satisfied; and if you of the Republican party do not really mean to aggress upon slavery where it now exists; if you are not, in fact, opposed to the admission of any more slave States; if, indeed, you do not any longer propose to use the powers of the Federal Government positively and aggressively to prohibit slavery in the Territories, but are satisfied to allow it to take its natural course, according to the laws of interest or of climate, then you, too, may well be content with this plan of adjustment, since it does not demand of you, openly and publicly, to deny, abjure, and renounce, in so many words, the more moderate principles and doctrines which you have this session professed. And yet, candor obliges me to declare, that this plan of settlement, and every other plan, whatsoever, which is of the slightest value—even the amendment of the gentleman from Massachuseets, [Mr. ADAMS,] is a virtual dissolution of the Republican party, as a mere sectional and anti-slavery organization; and this, too, will, in my judgment, be equally the result, whether we compromise at all, and the Union be thus restored, or whether it be finally and forever dissolved. The people of the North and the West will never trust the destroyers—for destroyers, indeed, you will be, if you reject all fair terms of adjustment—the destroyers of our Government, and such a Government as this, with the Administration and control of any other. You have now the executive department, as the result of the late election. Better, far better, reorganize and nationalize your party, and keep the Government for four years in peace, and with a Union of thirty-four States, than with the shadow and mockery of a broken and disjointed Union of sixteen or nineteen States, ending, at last, in total and hopeless dissolution.

Having thus, sir, guarded diligently the rights of the several States and sections, and given to each section also the power to protect itself inside of the Union from aggression, I propose next to limit and to regulate the alleged right of SECESSION, since this, from a dormant abstraction, has now become a practical question of tremendous import. As long, sir, as secession remained an untried and only menaced experiment, that confidence without which no Government can be stable or efficient, was not shaken, because it was believed that actual secession would never be tried; or if tried, that it must speedily and ingloriously fail. The popular faith, cherished for years, has been that the Union could not be dissolved. To that faith the Republican party was indebted for its success in the late election; and we who predicted its dissolution were smitten upon the cheek and condemned to feed upon bread of affliction and water of affliction, like the prophet whom Ahab hated. But partial dissolution has already occurred. Secession has been tried and has proved a speedy and a terrible success. The practicability of doing it and the way to do it, have both been established. Sir, the experiment may readily be repeated. It will be repeated. And is it not madness and folly, then, to call back, by adjustment, the States which have seceded, or to hold back the States which are threatening to secede, without providing some safeguard against the renewal of this most simple and disastrous experiment? Can foreign nations have any confidence hereafter in the stability of a Government which may so readily, speedily, and quietly be dissolved? Can we have any confidence among ourselves?

If it be said that it would have availed nothing to check secession in the Gulf States, even had there been a constitutional prohibition of it, I answer, perhaps not, if it had been total and absolute, for there would have been no alternative but submission or revolution; and hence I propose only to define and restrain and to regulate this alleged right. But I deny that, if a particular mode of secession had been prescribed by the Constitution, and thus every other mode prohibited, it would have been possible to have secured, in any of the seceding States—no, not even in South Carolina—a majority in favor of separate State secession, or secession in any other way than that provided in the Constitution. No, sir; it was the almost universal belief in the cotton States in the unlimited right of secession—a doctrine recognized by few in the free States, but held to by a great many, if not very generally, all over the slave States—which made secession so easy. It is hard to bring any considerable number of the people of the United States—suddenly, at least—up to the point of a palpable violation of the Constitution; but it is easy, very easy, to draw them into any act which seems to be only the exercise of one right for the purpose of securing and preserving the higher rights of life, liberty, person, and property for a whole State or a whole section. Sir, it is because of this very idea or notion among the people of the Gulf States, that they were exercising a right reserved under the Constitution, that secession there, and the establishment of a new confederacy and provisional government, have been marked by so much rapidity, order, and method, all through the ballot-box, and not with the halter, or at the point of the bayonet, over oppressed minorities; and, for the most part, with so few of the excesses and irregularities which have characterized the progress of other revolutions. I would not prohibit totally the right of secession, lest violent revolutions should follow; for where laws and constitutions are to be overleaped, and they who make the revolution avow it to be a revolution, and claim no right except the universal rights of man, such revolutions are commonly violent and bloody within themselves; and even if not, they cannot be resisted by the established authorities except at the cost of civil war; while, if submitted to in silence, they tend to demoralize all government. It is of vital importance, therefore, every way, in my judgment, that the exercise of this certainly *quasi* revolutionary right should be defined, limited, and restrained; and accordingly, I propose that no State shall secede without the consent of the Legislatures of all the States of the section to which the State proposing to secede may belong. This is obviously a most reasonable restraint; and yet, of its sufficiency no man can doubt, when he remembers that, in the present crisis of the country, had this provision existed, no State could have obtained the absolute consent, at least, of even one-half of the States of the South.

Such, Mr. Speaker, is the plan which, with great deference, and yet with great confidence, too, in its efficiency, I would propose for the adjustment of our controversies, and for the restoration and preservation of the Union which our fathers made. Like all human contrivances, certainly, it is imperfect, and subject to objection. But something searching, radical, extreme, going to the very foundations of government, and reaching the seat of the malady, must be done, and that right speedily, while the fracture is yet fresh and reunion is possible. Two months ago, when I last addressed the House, imploring you for immediate action, less, much less, would have sufficed; but we learned no wisdom from the lessons of the past; and now, indeed, not poppy, nor mandragora, nor other drowsy sirup is of any value to arrest that revolution, in the midst of which we are to-day—a revolution the grandest and the saddest of modern times.

# APPENDIX.

The following are the amendments to the Constitution proposed by Mr. VALLANDIGHAM:

## JOINT RESOLUTION.

Whereas the Constitution of the United States is a grant of specific powers delegated to the Federal Government by the people of the several States, all powers not delegated to it nor prohibited to the States being reserved to the States, respectively, or to the people; and whereas it is the tendency of stronger Governments to enlarge their powers and jurisdiction at the expense of weaker Governments, and of majorities to usurp and abuse power and oppress minorities, to arrest and hold in check which tendency compacts and constitutions are made; and whereas the only effectual constitutional security for the rights of minorities, whether as people or as States, is the power expressly reserved in constitutions of protecting those rights by their own action; and whereas this mode of protection by checks and guarantees is recognized in the Federal Constitution, as well in the case of the equality of the States in representation and in suffrage in the Senate, as in the provision for overruling the veto of the President and for amending the Constitution, not to enumerate other examples; and whereas, unhappily, because of the vast extent and diversified interests and institutions of the several States of the Union, sectional divisions can no longer be suppressed; and whereas it concerns the peace and stability of the Federal Union and Government that a division of the States into mere slaveholding and non-slaveholding sections, causing hitherto, and from the nature and necessity of the case, inflammatory and disastrous controversies upon the subject of slavery, ending already in present disruption of the Union, should be forever hereafter ignored; and whereas this important end is best to be obtained by the recognition of other sections without regard to slavery, neither of which sections shall alone be strong enough to oppress or control the others, and each be vested with the power to protect itself from aggressions: Therefore,

*Resolved by the Senate and House of Representatives of the United States of America in Congress assembled,* (two-thirds of both Houses concurring,) That the following articles be, and are hereby, proposed as amendments to the Constitution of the United States, which shall be valid to all intents and purposes as part of said Constitution when ratified by conventions in three-fourths of the several States:

### ARTICLE XIII.

SEC. 1. The United States are divided into four sections, as follows:

The States of Maine, New Hampshire, Vermont, Massachusetts, Rhode Island, Connecticut, New York, New Jersey, and Pennsylvania, and all new States annexed and admitted into the Union, or formed or erected within the jurisdiction of any of said States, or by the junction of two or more of the same, or of parts thereof, or out of territory acquired north of said States, shall constitute one section, to be known as the NORTH.

The States of Ohio, Indiana, Illinois, Michigan, Wisconsin, Minnesota, Iowa, and Kansas, and all new States annexed or admitted into the Union, or erected within the jurisdiction of any of said States, or by the junction of two or more of the same, or of parts thereof, or out of territory now held or hereafter acquired north of latitude 36° 30′, and east of the crest of the Rocky Mountains, shall constitute another section, to be known as the WEST.

The States of Oregon and California, and all new States annexed and admitted into the Union, or formed or erected within the jurisdiction of any of said States, or by the junction of two or more of the same, or of parts thereof, or out of territory now held or hereafter acquired west of the crest of the Rocky Mountains and of the Rio Grande, shall constitute another section, to be known as the PACIFIC.

The States of Delaware, Maryland, Virginia, North Carolina, South Carolina, Georgia, Florida, Alabama, Mississippi, Louisiana, Texas, Arkansas, Tennessee, Kentucky, and Missouri, and all new States annexed and admitted into the Union, or formed or erected within the jurisdiction of any of said States, or by the junction of two or more of the same, or of parts thereof, or out of territory acquired east of the Rio Grande and south of latitude 36° 30′, shall constitute another section, to be known as the SOUTH.

SEC. 2. On demand of one-third of the Senators of any one of the sections on any bill, order, resolution, or vote, to which the concurrence of the House of Representatives may be necessary, except on a question of adjournment, a vote shall be had by sections, and a majority of the Senators from each section voting shall be necessary to the passage of such bill, order, or resolution, and to the validity of every such vote.

SEC. 3. Two of the electors for President and Vice-President shall be appointed by each State in such manner as the Legislature thereof may direct, for the State at large. The other electors to which each State may be entitled, shall be chosen in the respective congressional districts into which the State may, at the regular decennial period, have been divided, by the electors of each district, having the qualifications requisite for electors of the most numerous branch of the State Legislature. A majority of all the electors in each of the four sections in this article established, shall be necessary to the choice of President and Vice-President; and the concurrence of a majority of the States of each section shall be necessary to the choice of President by the House of Representatives, and of the Senators from each section to the choice of Vice-President by the Senate, whenever the right of choice shall devolve upon them respectively.

SEC. 4. The President and Vice-President shall hold their office each during the term of six years; and neither shall be eligible to more than one term, except by the votes of two-thirds of all the electors of each section, or of the States of each section, whenever the right of choice of President shall devolve upon the House of Representatives, or of Senators from each section whenever the right of choice of Vice-President shall devolve upon the Senate.

SEC. 5. The Congress shall by law provide for the case of failure by the House of Representatives to choose a President, and of the Senate to choose a Vice-President, whenever the right of choice shall devolve upon them respectively, declaring what officer sha'l then act as President; and such officer shall act accordingly until a President shall be elected. The Congress shall also provide by law for a special election for President and Vice-President in such case to be held and completed within six months from the expiration of the term of office of the last preceding President, and to be conducted in all respects as provided for in the Constitution for regular elections of the same officer, except that if the House of Representatives shall not choose a President, should the right of choice devolve upon them, within twenty days from the opening of the certificates and counting of the electoral votes, then the Vice-President shall act as President, as in the case of the death or other constitutional disability of the President. The term of office of the President chosen under such special election shall continue six years from the fourth day of March preceding such election.

ARTICLE XIV.

No State shall secede without the consent of the Legislatures of the States of the section to which the State proposing to secede belongs. The President shall have power to adjust with seceding States all questions arising by reason of their secession; but the terms of adjustment shall be submitted to the Congress for their approval before the same sha'l be valid.

ARTICLE XV.

Neither the Congress nor a Territorial Legislature shall have power to interfere with the right of the citizens of any of the States within either of the sections to migrate upon equal terms with the citizens of the States within either of the other sections to the Territories of the United States: nor shall either the Congress or a Territorial Legislature have power to destroy or impair any rights of either person or property in the Territories.

New States annexed for admission into the Union, or formed or erected within the jurisdiction of other States, or by the junction of two or more States, or parts of States; and States formed, with the consent of the Congress, out of any territory of the United States, shall be entitled to admission upon an equal footing with the original States, under any constitution establishing a government republican in form which the people thereof may ordain, whenever such States, if formed out of any territory of the United States, shall contain, within an area of not less than sixty thousand square miles, a population equal to the then existing ratio of representation for one member of the House of Representatives.

---

A card, from which the following is extracted, was published by Mr. VALLANDIGHAM in the *Cincinnati Enquirer*, on the 10th of November, 1860—a few days after the presidential election:

"And now let me add that I did say, not in Washington, not at a dinner-table, not in the presence of 'fire-eaters,' but in the City of New York, in public assembly of northern men, and in a public speech at the Cooper Institute, on the 2d of November, 1860, that, 'if any one or more of the States of this Union should, at any time, secede—for reasons of the sufficiency and justice of which, before God and the great tribunal of history, they alone may judge—much as I should deplore it, *I never would, as a Representative in the Congress of the United States, vote one dollar of money whereby one drop of American blood should be shed in a civil war.*' That sentiment, thus uttered in the presence of thousands of the merchants and solid men of the free and patriotic city of New York, was received with vehement and long-continued applause, the entire vast assemblage rising as one man and cheering for some minutes. And I now deliberately repeat and reaffirm it, resolved, though I stand alone, though all others yield and fall away, to make it good to the last moment of my public life. No menace, no public clamor, no taunts, nor sneers, nor foul detraction, from any quarter, shall drive me from my firm purpose. Ours is a Government of opinion, not of force; a Union of free will, not arms; and coercion is civil war; a war of sections, a war of States, waged by a race compounded and made up of all other races; full of intellect, of courage, of will unconquerable, and, when set on fire by passion, the most belligerent and most ferocious on the globe; a civil war full of horrors, which no imagination can conceive and no pen portray. If Abraham Lincoln is wise, looking truth and danger full in the face, he will take counsel of the 'old men,' the moderates of his party, and advise peace, negotiation, concession; but if like the foolish son of the wise king, he reject these wholesome counsels, and hearken only to the madmen who threaten chastisement with scorpions, let him see to it, lest it be recorded at last that none remained to serve him 'save the house of Judah only.' At least, if he will forget the secession of the Ten Tribes, will he not remember and learn a lesson of wisdom from the secession of the Thirteen Colonies?"

www.ingramcontent.com/pod-product-compliance
Lightning Source LLC
LaVergne TN
LVHW011145110826
845150LV00008B/2510
* 9 7 8 1 4 1 8 1 9 2 0 5 1 *